The Libertarian Party Versus Liberty

By

Robert Villegas

The Libertarian Party versus Liberty

By Robert Villegas

ISBN-13: 978-1539557531

ISBN-10: 1539557537

Social Media Addresses

Parler: @Robertv1989
CloutHub @RobertVillegas
MeWe www.mewe.com/i/robertvillegas
Minds @Robertv1989
Gab @V4Vendata
GETTR @V4Vendata
WIMKIN Robert Villegas
Freetalk45 @V4Vendata
Spreely @V4Vendata

Table of Contents

Introduction

It is an interesting phenomenon that university-derived ideologies have been relegated to the status of the "not to be mentioned" in political campaigns. The reason for this is that politicians think their advocacy of a specific ideology would mean they would not get many votes. So rather than openly appealing to their ideology, they declare pragmatism and a "dedication" to "the real world".

Pragmatism is the philosophy that guides these politicians because an appeal to formal ideologies would be unpopular. Rather than declare fealty to communism, socialism, and fascism, politicians appeal to "practical action". This hides their true ideologies for which they continue to work nonetheless. Pragmatism countenances that they only talk about "practical" solutions to "solving" real problems when in fact, these discussions are actually about communism, socialism, and fascism. This fallacy only means they don't care if their policies fail; they only care whether they get elected or not.

However, the trend of avoiding ideology is not reserved to statist progressives like Hillary Clinton.

Conservatives, to a large extent, don't want people to know they favor a theological form of government which is why they too advance the idea that they are pragmatists. If the public were to know this, they too might lose votes.

Another group hiding its ideological bent is the Libertarian Party. If the public were to know that this party was made up of anarchists, it would likely not get many votes. So, we must conclude that conservatives and libertarians are part of the pragmatist trend in America.

In view of this anti-ideological bent among politicians and CEOs, there is every reason to fear the advent of fascism. Both Hillary Clinton, Joe Biden, and Donald Trump favor bigger government that will encroach further on the rights and lives of individuals. Those limited government advocates in the Libertarian Party can only serve the interests of fascism if they continue to support a party that has subversive intentions. It shall be the purpose of this short book to show why the LP cannot succeed and to offer an approach toward liberty that will work.

The Libertarian Party

"The Libertarian party was founded in Colorado in 1971 and held its first convention in Denver in 1972. In 1972 it fielded John Hospers for president and Theodora Nathan for vice president in the U.S. general election. It appeared on two state ballots, receiving a total of 2,648 votes in Colorado and Washington. In the 1976 elections, the party's 176 candidates garnered 1.2 million votes across the United States."[1] Before that they were little known and struggling to develop the narratives they needed to support Libertarian ideas.

Still, even now, many people think the libertarian movement is a distinctly American movement fostering liberty and "American values". On the contrary, the Libertarian Party is merely faux American in principle. "The Libertarian party views government as both the cause and the effect of social ills.

"The Libertarian party promotes the ABOLITION of compulsory military service, government control of television and other media, laws regarding sexual activity between consenting adults, laws

[1] https://usapoliticaldatabase.weebly.com/history-of-the-libertarians.html

against the use of mood-altering substances, and government control of migration and immigration. Under its leadership farming quotas and subsidies would be eliminated, there would be no mandatory schooling and no MINIMUM WAGE, and defense spending would be drastically reduced. According to the party, the form of government it promotes would be less expensive than the current system of federal, state, and local governance."[2]

The libertarian movement was originally thought to be an extension of Ayn Rand's philosophy of Objectivism. Ms. Rand disagreed vociferously with libertarianism, and she strove to distance herself from the movement. Her view was that America needed a new philosophy of man not a distinctly political movement. She sought the establishment of an intellectual revolution where "new intellectuals" engaged in the arduous work of convincing people that a new metaphysics and epistemology was necessary. It was too early for a new political movement, she argued.

Capitalism is an economic system based upon the principle of individual rights. Without individual

---

[2] Ibid

rights, Rand argued, there is no capitalism. Capitalism is not what happens when there is no government. It is not what happens in the jungle or wilderness. It is not what happened during primitive tribal periods. Capitalism can only happen when there is a philosophical context of ideas that recognizes how man survives in society and how a society should be structured.

Individual rights define the limits of interaction and trade among individuals in society. Fundamentally, capitalism is founded upon the idea that man functions and survives by means of reason. Reason is the means by which man's mind ascertains reality; it leads to the accomplishment of values in a social context not the least of which are happiness, affluence, and freedom.

In order for capitalism to be achieved, a consistent intellectual movement must take place, one based in reason, and possessing a clarity of ideas. An intellectual situation must be achieved wherein the concept of man's rights is generally understood, accepted, and implemented in terms of the proper form of government. A government is the institution in society that implements the rules of interaction among men and ensures that the laws of society are followed. Because of this, those who choose to work toward the establishment of a proper government must be fully consistent. Further, they must not join forces with others who advocate opposing systems of government.

Liberty is a political concept that identifies man's right to live for his own sake. Liberty is the political expression of a long chain of reasoning that starts with the importance of free will in the life of man and proceeds to a declaration that man has fundamental rights which derive from his means of survival – and that in order to achieve survival and happiness, he must be free politically to engage in those actions which result in his success. Liberty also implies that all (or most) men in society deal with each other by means of reason and persuasion with force effectively outlawed. The discussion leading up to government concludes that a constitutionally limited government not only protects man's rights but also uses force (according to objectively defined standards) to capture and punish law breakers. Liberty is not possible without objective law and a limited government.

Yet, the term "liberty" is not an expression of a legal/political concept by any means. It is, in a sense, a value that expresses a general desire of men to be left alone. Liberty means freedom but is not, in itself, a political expression in the legal sense. When I say, "I want liberty", I mean that I want to be left alone by government. But the means for accomplishing liberty is the protection of individual rights, meaning limited government.

Some people associate the term liberty, the desire to be left alone, with the absence of government altogether. But this cannot be true. The concept liberty does not exist in the primitive jungle. Certainly, living in the jungle has sometimes meant living freely, without restriction, but this is not the same thing as liberty. Liberty is an intellectual development, an abstraction that comes about only in a social context. In fact, the primitive environment, whenever societies develop, tends to be tribal and collectivist in nature. Liberty is not possible in such an environment when men are struggling to eke out a living against the oppression of nature. Liberty has no place in such an environment because ideas don't exist in nature; principles do.

In our present circumstance, the term "liberty" is being coopted by a group of people who have an entirely different society in mind. The term, "libertarianism" is an epistemological package deal that many (innocently) think refers to an advocacy of liberty but, in fact, openly refers to anarchism. As Dr. Leonard Peikoff pointed out in 2012, libertarianism is presented as "a viewpoint, as a theory, as an ideology and as such, ... it is intrinsically invalid to make the term "liberty" into a theory or ideology. You cannot take (an) out of context value and add "ism" to it and make a legitimate position out of it; an intellectual position."[3] (Parenthesis mine)

Dr. Peikoff is talking about a group of people who claim to advocate liberty, yet who have not specifically defined the fundamental principles that support the concept. The term "liberty" is too broad to be the foundation of an intellectual movement. It is a term that leaves open the type of government that would secure liberty in a social context. To be a libertarian could mean that one advocates either limited government or anarchocapitalism, the latter of which is a meaningless term. It is ambiguous, to say the least; but any compromise between the two terms could

---

3   http://www.peikoff.com/2012/10/22/a-discussion-with-yaron-brook-on-libertarianism/

put limited government advocates in league with their own opposition.

The result of this compromise is that men lose the right of specificity when it comes to the critical question of the proper type of government. This fundamental division makes libertarianism into a fringe element in society. It cannot break into the mainstream because most people reject the concept of anarchism.

Rand versus Rothbard

The history of anarchism has been one of disrespect for the foundations of society, of hatred for law, and of superficial sentimentality based upon a professed love for nature; all propped up by any philosophical statement amenable to the view that all governments should be destroyed. Anarchism holds that there should be no governmental authority, in short, no government. In this sense, the concept of liberty can be applied to it, but the concept of limited government cannot.

Anarchocapitalists cannot be dissociated from historical anarchism, since their position that all governments are evil comprises the main feature upon which all variations of anarchism are based. Classical anarchists, those who lived around the time of the Industrial Revolution, were born of a time when man's intelligence and labor were beginning to achieve a maximization of effort unprecedented in human history.

In the midst of this extraordinary progress, the anarchists offered nothing more than an organic harmony with nature. They were rejected by those who knew that property, law, and production were essential to human survival and happiness. People did not have the time nor the desire to rebuild society all over again, by means of destroying the infrastructure and political institutions that had given them abundance and prosperity.

One of the ancient anarchists, Callicles of Acharnae, a Greek from the late 5th Century B.C., basing his arguments on the Sophist position that might makes right, held that laws were made by weak men, in order to control and restrain the few who were strong. The Greek poet, Pindar, held that 'natural justice," rid of the impediment of laws, would result in a situation when might would be right. These Greek arguments, with their disrespect for voluntary consent and productive effort, do not represent the stated views of today's anarchocapitalists. The concept of "natural justice," as used by the Sophists, is simply too anti-social a concept for modern-day anarchists. Their version of natural justice holds that a free, efficient, and highly advanced technological society would result from anarchy. In the anarchocapitalist scheme, production makes right.

The Sophists were more realistic about the outcome of a government-less society. What anarchocapitalists neglect is that throughout historical times man has been the same biological entity with the same characteristic method of survival. In order for the Sophist position to be wrong, and the anarchocapitalist position right, a new man must have come on the scene, a man so constituted that he commit violence under no circumstances. No such new man has arisen, and the same laws apply to modern man that applied during Sophist times. In short, without government to protect man's rights, might would rule.

During the 1930s, Ayn Rand came into the discussion. This Russian immigrant had experienced directly the squalor and decline that Marxist (and later progressive) ideas brought about. Not only did she hate the Soviet Union, she also testified that it was a big lie. Her novel, Atlas Shrugged changed the conversation and exposed the corruption of the left so eloquently that she developed an instant following among people who were not afraid to take on the "altruism establishment". Yet, she also found a significant opposition among many liberals and conservatives who were deeply invested in the philosophy of plunder. These became her enemies.

Others, a small minority, realized that Rand's views were not merely economic arguments for capitalism but philosophic as well. She offered a full system that she later called Objectivism. This philosophy offered a fully-defined metaphysics, epistemology, ethics, politics, and aesthetic. Yet, many people were not looking for this and took her politics out of context and began using her arguments for capitalism without the full philosophical context. They expropriated her arguments for freedom and individual rights without reference to her views on atheism, the nature of reality and man's need for reason. Some even tried to bolster conservativism using her economic principles while focusing only on the cause and effect between capitalism and prosperity.

Some intellectuals, those mostly wedded to alternative, out-of-the-mainstream views, saw only the economic argument and wanted to use it to advance their own political perspective. They didn't care so much about metaphysics and epistemology and were, in essence, amoral (pragmatist) when it came to values. They extracted her economic views from her philosophy and thought they could create a new movement without moral judgment. Latching on to pragmatist economists like Ludwig von Mises, they appropriated a Kantian-based economic and political framework called praxeology and claimed to be followers of Ayn Rand (who rejected Mises' praxeology).

These people began to call themselves libertarians and sought to create a movement out of the foundation of both Mises' and Ayn Rand's economic principles but without her philosophical principles. Many of these pragmatists thought that a political approach could succeed because, they felt, the American people implicitly liked capitalism if only they could be reminded of its value. Some even thought that Rand would welcome the movement. Many hoped she would drop the context of her philosophical views and back the libertarian political movement. They were wrong.

In 1974, she wrote to a fan:

"...I am profoundly opposed to today's so-called libertarian movement and to the theories of Dr. Murray Rothbard. So-called libertarians are my avowed enemies, yet I've heard many reports on their attempts to cash in on my name and mislead my readers into the exact opposite of my views.

"Please call to your daughter's attention my article "The Nature of Government," in my book *Capitalism: The Unknown Ideal.*"[4]

In this article, she writes:

"A government is an institution that holds the exclusive power to *enforce* certain rules of social conduct in a given geographical area.

"Do men need such an institution—and why?

"Since man's mind is his basic tool of survival, his means of gaining knowledge to guide his actions—the basic condition he requires is the freedom to think and to act according to his rational judgment. This does not mean that a man must live alone and that a desert island is the environment best suited to his needs. Men can derive enormous benefits from dealing with one another. A social environment is most conducive to their successful survival—*but only on certain conditions...*"[5]

What would make a civil society destructive of man's successful survival? It would have to be a

---

[4] The Letters of Ayn Rand The Later Years (1960-1981)

[5] Capitalism: The Unknown Ideal by Ayn Rand Appendix: The Nature of Government

society that mixes coercion with freedom, what some call a mixed economy. It would be one that re-distributes income from producers to non-producers. It would be a society that intervenes in the economic affairs of people and gives money and power to government cronies and beneficiaries.

Murray Rothbard, one of the founders of anarchocapitalism, had indicated a significant interest in the ideas of Ayn Rand and he joined her circle for a time. More than likely, they parted over disagreements in which Rand had a wider perspective philosophically. Judging from reports, Rothbard was highly critical of the people in her circle and believed that Rand represented a cult.

Yet, the real issue seemed to be that Rand would not accept the idea of natural rights that Rothbard attributed to her. In addition, his statement that Rand's ideas were not original missed the innovations Rand made about some important philosophical questions. Rand was not trying to copy other philosophers and call it her original work. She gave full credit to other philosophers when she agreed with them, but she clearly drew the lines between her ideas and those who ignored wider philosophical issues.

Rothbard appears to have made a fairly shallow assessment of Rand's ideas and (in effect) declared his own perspective superior to hers. Rand cannot be lumped in with other philosophers because her ideas stand on their own while other current thinkers are steeped in modern philosophy which Rand had repudiated. Philosophically, one cannot make a cursory assessment of a full philosophic statement (without understanding that statement) and be considered astute by any means. I suspect that one could not sit in a room with Ayn Rand and bring up other thinkers without her understanding the full implications that, they themselves, missed.

For instance, his assertion that Rand had introduced him to natural law and natural rights philosophy was a misinterpretation of her views. Rand actually held that man's rights were inherent in his nature as a being who survived by means of his mind (through reason). She did not hold nature, as such, as a starting point for ideas like individual rights. She was not a conservative. Dr. Peikoff explains:

"Natural law is not a feature superimposed by some agency on an otherwise "chaotic" world; there is no possibility of such chaos. Nor is there any possibility of a "chance" event, if "chance" means an exception to causality. Cause and effect is not a metaphysical afterthought. It is not a fact that is theoretically dispensable. It is part of the fabric of reality as such.

"One may no more ask: who is responsible for natural law (which amounts to asking: who caused causality?) than one may ask: who created the universe? The answer to both questions is the same: existence exists."[6]

I've often thought that the idea of "natural rights" is misleading. The term nature normally refers to the forms of cause and effect that result in the growth of living things or in the physical laws that create actions of certain types. When it comes to the actions of men, it is not about nature as such but about the free will that men have – free will is not a natural phenomenon that operates according to fixed laws (determinism). Man has choices and none of those choices are natural in the determinist sense.

As Bacon said, "Nature, to be commanded, must be obeyed." This reflects the proper relationship between nature and man. Man is not determined;

---

[6] Objectivism; the Philosophy of Ayn Rand by Dr. Leonard Peikoff Chapter 1 Reality

he is not a fixed follower of nature but of his own mind.

Man must choose to gain the knowledge necessary for survival by understanding nature. Likewise, the question of whether to use reason is also a choice. There are no "natural laws" or "natural rights" when it comes to man; there is only free will. Rights are a recognition of the fact that man can only survive by exercising reason (by choosing to think) and then acting to accomplish his goals and values.

To say that something is "necessary", when it comes to a creature with free will, is not the same as saying it is compulsory or that it is determined. With man, the discovery of the necessary conditions for survival does not imply that man must implement those conditions – only that he *should* implement them if he wants survival. It does not imply that nature requires them; only that there are necessary conditions if man wants to live an affluent and successful life. Morality is, after all, a "normative" science.

Likewise, to say that "nature" consists of certain processes which are necessary according to the rules of physics (let's say) is quite a different thing from saying that man has a certain nature that requires a certain type of society. The confusion here is in equating "physical" nature with the idea of human nature. One is necessary in reality; the other is dependent upon man's choice.

In this sense, man has two options. There is the option which consists of his potentiality for the best and highest mind as well as the option to refuse to seek that highest mind; in short, to refuse to think. Neither of these two options is "natural" in the sense that we normally think of the term. They are not determined by nature because of the element of choice.

Man doesn't reason automatically in the way that animals pursue survival automatically. Man has to choose to think because he has the ability to go beyond the natural into the reasonable. And this is clearly not the same as "natural law" or "natural rights". Yet, the principle of free will is applicable to man whereas the idea of "natural law" is not determined by any means.

The key distinction here is the assumption that if man is free to survive, as he would be in nature, then an affluent capitalist system would be the necessary result. It is this notion of some automatically determined capitalist system (as an outgrowth of nature) that is the key to Rothbard's contradiction. Ideas do not create themselves, and neither do economic systems. Men use their conceptual abilities to create ideas. Those ideas arise within an intellectual context, a chronological order that develops hierarchically and only starting from a foundation of "what is".

Likewise, the idea that there are natural rights is also a contradiction of the same sort. Nature does not operate conceptually. It does not invent abstractions such as individual rights; those are created by men as part of an intellectual/conceptual development. Nature does not create capitalism – men's thoughts and knowledge create the ideas that define and create society.

Rothbard's own leanings indicate a clear departure from the ideas of Ayn Rand (and more than likely, this departure existed before they were ever introduced) – which would have served to isolate Rothbard among those in her group. It was not a cult he was up against but human minds thinking rationally.

Such thinkers as Spooner, Godwin, Proudhon and many others developed a variety of anarchist tenets which, for the most part, advocated some form of "natural law" or "natural rights. The basic premise of most of these thinkers is that reason and its advance in society would eventually erase the need for government. But this view (almost Marxist in spirit) ignores the basic fact that reason is optional and that each individual is born tabula rasa without a "nature-determined" reasoning ability. Man must first be taught how to reason and secondly, he must choose to exert that ability throughout every decision he makes. Although a society that values reason, teaches it and builds its institutions around it, would certainly be a better society, there is no possibility that all men will choose to make the effort to use reason. It is similar to the distinction between the mover and the moved in physics; at any given time, some units are moved, and some others are movers. Likewise, with reason, at any given time, some men are thinkers and others are intellectually passive. Society does not tend toward reason any more than a stationary billiard ball tends toward motion.

Much in the same way that Hegel believed that the thesis-antithesis-synthesis process was predictive of human movements, many anarchists held to a form of "spontaneous order" to predict human movements. In fact, the mere "assertion" of such an "order" is predictive of nothing. There is no spontaneous principle that will expunge the need for government – there is no such natural law that brings about the types of society men will create. And, even more importantly, there is no guarantee that, once a given type of society is established, that it will, by any natural (or determined) means, sustain itself in that form. All such societies are dependent upon man's free will, his choice to structure society in the way he decides and the methods of thinking he will use in his every-day activities.

Additionally, throughout the history of philosophy, there have been several views on the nature of reason. The psychology or inclinations of a given philosopher can be so convoluted that it is possible for very bad ideas to dominate despite the fact that they proclaim reason. A society that proclaims reason can still be antithetical to reason. Examples are Kant, Hume and several other "dead ends" that have had disastrous consequences for men.

The upshot is that the battle for reason represents one of man's most complex endeavors and history has shown that we are far from discovering it as a society.

In a sense, the various forms of anarchism that have been put forward represent what I call "piggy-back" philosophies which latch on to the selective implications of other forms of thought. Anarchists have been collectivists, individualists, communists and virtually every shade of "ism" from far left to far right. This is an indication that the foundations of anarchism are not "nature", as they claim, and that anarchism will take on any color so long as it can insinuate itself into a group of people and exert influence by means of other principles. With so many rationalizations, then, it is not surprising that so few mainstream intellectuals have bought into the idea of a government-less society. The anarchists have merely been "hangers-on" who hope for a major movement that will deal them in. The rest is just smoke and mirrors.

For instance, some believed that the natural order was self-sacrificing collectivism while others believed it was individualism and even capitalism. They all held that either government would wither away or that anarchy, no government, would produce a utopian end. None of this is possible on those terms.

Aristotle informs us that the term "archai" refers essentially to governments, "That from which a thing can first be known, this also is called the beginning of a thing..."[7] The term "anarchy" then is an absence of government, most often associated with times of chaos, revolution, and social breakdown. Needless to say, some people have argued for these situations; we see them sometimes on the streets throwing rocks through shop windows. They want destruction because they are essentially nihilists and have a problem with the very concept of social order or capitalism.

Yet, the crux of the issue for most anarchists is their Kantian base. Most anarchists hold that man is an imperfect being incapable of knowing how to act in a world about which they have imperfect knowledge. This view precludes the possibility of reason and leads them to nihilism which is the desire to destroy. Most anarchists avoid the centrality of this viewpoint and ignore the fact that

---

[7] Aristotle Compete Works Kindle version Book V Part. 1

anarchism represents a metaphysical break from reality which leads them to blindly advocate anything that denigrates or destroys society. They especially seek the destruction of societies that protect and advance man's ability to live by means of his mind. They are in perennial conflict with all aspects of human society and all men, rational and irrational, which is why anarchists must always be revolutionaries and enemies of any form of society. They are more prone to latch onto "isms" which require destruction of some type because these "isms" are a means to their end which is destruction. Hence, you see them making common cause with communists, fascists, revolutionary feminists, leftists, deconstructionists, nihilists, and fanatics of a wide variety.

Anarchocapitalism

With the advent of capitalism and particularly the arguments of such intellectuals as Mises and Hayak to name a few, a new group of anarchists, the libertarians, claimed that capitalism was the closest thing to nature; in other words, the condition that exists without the presence of man. The argument goes like this: if capitalism brings about affluence and prosperity, the natural order, then capitalism does not need government. Capitalism has its own natural order that is made up of the law of supply and demand. In capitalism, people will want to be defended against criminals so they will create a demand for defense services which will be more efficient than government (because government is always inefficient).

But capitalism does not bring about a natural order of this type. A natural order is "physical" or "necessary" and has nothing to do with a society created by a philosophical stream of development. One cannot start by creating society (capitalism) and then claim that it will bring about "nature" or "natural rights". It won't happen because, hierarchically, one idea cannot bring about ideas upon which it depends and chronologically it cannot wipe out ideas that it upholds. Hence, anarchocapitalism is not a true "ism" because it is an impossibility – an inner contradiction.

Anarchocapitalism is a view invented by Murray Rothbard who is also considered one of the founders of the libertarian movement and Party. In a speech entitled "Society without a State," Rothbard began:

"In attempting to outline how a society without a state—i.e. an anarchist society—might function successfully, I would like to defuse two common but mistaken criticisms of the approach. First is the argument that in providing for such defense or protection services as courts, police, or even law itself, I am merely smuggling the state back into society in another form, and that therefore the system I am both analyzing and advocating is not 'really' anarchism. This sort of criticism can only involve us in an endless and arid dispute over semantics. Let me say from the beginning that I define the state as that institution which possesses one or both (almost always both) of the following properties: (I) it acquires its income by the physical coercion known as 'taxation'; and (2) it asserts and usually obtains a coerced monopoly of the provision of defense services (police and courts) over a given territorial area. Any institution not possessing either of these properties is not and cannot be, in accordance with my definition, a 'state.'"

This last is true. Such a society is anarchy but the definition of anarchy is not simply a state of peace without government as Rothbard implies. There is no peace in anarchy at any time and by any means except the peace that exists after one army totally annihilates another. Anarchy is, in effect, the absence of government. It holds government up as an entity that men can do without under the premise that it the state which annihilates men for the sake of plunder – and that government can only be against men.

In response to a question from a fan about the Libertarian Party, Ayn Rand wrote:

"Do not "proselytize" indiscriminately, i.e., do not force discussions or arguments on those who are not interested or not willing to argue. It is not your job to save everyone's soul. If you do the things which are in your power, you will not feel guilty about not doing—"somehow"—the things which are not.

"Above all, do not join the wrong *ideological* groups or movements, in order to "do something." By "ideological" (in this context), I mean groups or movements proclaiming some vaguely generalized, undefined (and, usually, contradictory) *political* goals. (E.g., the Conservative Party, that subordinates reason to faith, and substitutes theocracy for capitalism; or the "libertarian" hippies, who subordinate reason to whims, and substitute anarchism for capitalism.) To join such groups means to reverse the philosophical hierarchy and to sell out fundamental principles for the sake of some superficial political action which is bound to fail. It means that you help the defeat of *your* ideas and the victory of your enemies. (For a discussion of the reasons, see "The Anatomy of Compromise" in my book *Capitalism:* The *Unknown* Ideal.)"

"The only groups one may properly join today are ad hoc committees, i.e., groups organized to achieve a single, specific, clearly defined goal, on which men of differing views can agree. In such cases, no one may attempt to ascribe his views to the entire membership, or to use the group to serve some hidden ideological purpose (and *this* has to be watched very, very vigilantly)."[8]

Notice that Rand starts her discussion by looking at reality while Rothbard has constructed a conceptual framework based upon a definition. This last is a hallmark of rationalism, the process of basing one's argument on floating abstractions disconnected from a body of knowedge rooted in reality.

Anarchists start with a floating abstraction which, as Rand says, substitutes anarchism for capitalism, stealing the traits of capitalism and ascribing them to anarchism. This is the sleight of hand that libertarians attempt – but they go even further. They seek to silence those among them who advocate limited government.

Rand's response is focused on the real. She wants to discuss real issues not an impossible concept such as "a society without a state" which approaches the issue in mid-stream after laying down several false and unreal constructs. The question, properly is not "should we or should we not have a

---

[8] The Ayn Rand Letter Vol. 1, No. 7 January 3, 1972 "What Can One Do?"

government?" but "what does man require in order to live in society?"

Since, in a free-market, the positive or good is allowed to predominate, they think that because of their advocacy of a free market without government, they (the libertarians) must be the most consistent free-market advocates in history. And this is the problem with coming at solutions mid-stream; you are now able to claim that those who come at it from fundamentals are the faulty thinkers; they are discriminatory and violating fundamental principles.

Yet, the fundamental principle, when it comes to defining a proper society, is not anarchy held in a vacuum; it is individual rights which derives from the need of man to use reason in order to survive. A society without government cannot defend individual rights because it provides no physical mechanism for that defense – no police. Anarchists pretend to defend freedom and liberty, but they ignore the fundamental need to base rights on an objective standard that is founded on governmentally organized defense.

Anarchy is an absence of government. It is not a fundamental principle. It is a derivative concept arrived at by faulty logic. An anarchistic condition of society cannot defend individual rights. In fact, freedom cannot be accomplished in a vacuum. In the absence of limited government, freedom cannot be accomplished at all – only chaos can.

Freedom (liberty) can only be established after the creation of an intellectual framework of ideas that are rooted in reality. Men act in reality, but their rights only exist if other men honor them, recognize them, and understand them. Rights do not come from nature or the free market; they come from man's mind as it observes reality.

Limited government is not statism, but the only system in history devised to replace it. The central focus of limited government is man's volitional nature, and its purpose is to protect man's right to make his own decisions and rational actions. Only on this basis can a clear understanding of limited government be obtained.

If one isolates the concept government, in order to find its essential function, one finds the singular: monopoly on defense services. The only other function possible to a government is offense. But a group engaged in coercion and no defense of rights is not a government, but a mob of gangsters engaged in general looting. Further, gangsters who want to obtain a monopoly on their coercive activities, in order to protect their scheme, would need to provide defense services for those who might otherwise be victimized by rival gangs. This distinction is important to bear in mind, because it provides the clue to just what Rothbard tried to pull.

Rothbard was right when he maintained that his speculation on defense agencies did not smuggle in government. In order to smuggle in government, he would have had to advocate a monopoly on force. One can charge, however, that his definition of a state was imprecise since it did not clearly name the fundamentals involved.

Rothbard's definition ensured (rationalistically) that the generally regarded model of limited government fell under the category of 'state'.

The use of taxation as one of the conditions necessary for statism was itself a matter of semantics. Certainly, any government that acquires its income by taxation has that aspect of statism, but this is not, by itself, a proof that the total system is statist. For instance, a limited government could have a voluntary tax system while a statist system would never allow such a thing.

If we are to advocate for the proper type of government, rather than debate the useless issue of whether government is necessary at all, we must know that anarchism is not an option. We must understand the nature of government and why we need it.

How not to Fight for Political Freedom

In my early youth I had developed a great admiration for the leaders of the American Revolution. Their courageous and uncompromising stands regarding for liberty revealed to me the greatness men of principle can muster in times of trouble. I had also become increasingly amazed at the tide of prosperity that the establishment of their political principles had released upon the world. Their United States of America had become the greatest nation on earth.

In those early days, I developed a pattern of thinking unlike many of the youngsters around me. Instead of running from the ideas of liberty, self-sufficiency, and individual achievement. I welcomed them and strove to be like those men whose greatness had been responsible for so much good.

Later, I learned that the attitudes of my fellow youngsters were part of a wider and different pattern of thinking. Amorality had crept into the fiber of our society to such an extent, and with such overwhelming approval, that in my time, the principles of man's rights had become mere rhetoric in the politician's and educator's arsenal of deception. Indeed, I thought, the time had arrived for a resurrection of principle and a re-dedication to the power of self-sufficiency. I resolved to do what I could to bring about such a change.

Then, in my early twenties, I discovered that I was not alone in my opinions regarding liberty. Other people were dedicated to the struggle to liberate man. A small group called the libertarians was writing away, virtually ignored by most people. I began subscribing to their publications, and vowed my support. I began calling myself a libertarian.

But enthusiasm was not enough. I was simply not clear on principle. I did not realize that on critical issues like man's rights only the right approach works. I discovered that these same libertarians, these guardians of liberty, had become mere political opportunists.

The Founding Fathers, as principled as they were, were not fanatics, and above all, compromise on liberty was out of the question. Further, they knew enough about ideas to realize that their time was right, that liberty was popular and possible. I learned that the libertarians, as fighters for liberty, stand like misguided school children by comparison.

Needless to say, I no longer call myself a libertarian. I have chosen to wage my battle for liberty under the banner of the intellect and with the pen as my tool; a tool that seeks no compromise.

I am certain that many people will take issue with me over my refusal to promote libertarianism or join the party. But I would like to cite a few lines from just one article in order to make clear the unreasonableness of the political approach taken by most libertarians. It is called "The L.P. Convention" by Murray N. Rothbard. It appeared in Rothbard's newsletter, The Libertarian Forum, September, 1975.

The article began with jubilant generalities about the Party Convention held Labor Day weekend, 1975, in New York City. Rothbard qualified his jubilation however, by stating that "It was the best of times; it was the worst of times; it was a week of highs and lows, a cauldron of love and hate;"

Most party conventions are characterized by divisiveness, and one wouldn't assume that Rothbard's statement refers to anything of major consequence, at least not for a Libertarian Party, one whose members agreed on so many fundamentals. But we shall see what developed.

Rothbard next recalled what he saw as the goals of the new L.P. leadership. These goals consist of making the Libertarian Party more attractive to the general populace. Philosophical discussion is important, but we must first reach those people 'who would flock to our standard if they were only able to learn of our existence.'

Rothbard apparently believed, even back then, that there were many people already philosophically convinced about libertarian principles, but who simply did not know about Libertarianism. This was a miscalculation. Practically everything about our society at the time was in total neglect of the fundamentals which make up a free society. Indeed, most arguments for freedom were either hip versions based on egalitarianism or the dried-up mess of conservatism. There was no flock because there had not been enough philosophical groundwork laid, enough philosophical discussion of the principles that needed to be accepted by a great majority before a Libertarian Party could take power. In fact, just two years after Rothbard wrote, we elected Jimmy Carter who was far from a libertarian. Then we elected Reagan to clean up the mess, but the nation did not elect enough of a majority for him to be effective in slowing down the growth of government – even if he wanted to do it. Then there was Bush, more or less, a liberal, Clinton, a liberal and the Bush 2 who grew the government even more than Clinton. It was only during liberal progressive Obama that a minority Tea Party rose up but this group was far from libertarian – more limited government in nature.

Even today, the principles left to us by the Founding Fathers have been so totally discredited by today's intelligentsia that the philosophical discussion thus far done by libertarians, particularly since it is being done so inadequately, amounts to so many school boys' spit balls by comparison.

By philosophical discussion, I am not talking about sitting in the living rooms of friends and engaging in give and take about liberty. I'm talking about the kind of discussion that is engaged in by professors and educators of all sorts, people who mold the future by clearly teaching the principles that validate and make up a proper society. The entire society must be saturated with the discussion about what is a proper society and how to bring it about. We don't get this from Rothbard's or today's libertarians.

Even now, after 48 years of the Libertarian Party, the political approach is merely so much wasted effort. When one considers that Soviet-style brutality may be days away, there is no alternative to waging a proper philosophical battle while there is time to do so. Public relations and vague political principles pose no great threat to the advance of statism. In fact, without a clearly articulated defense of liberty, the libertarians will be taken as part of a much larger right-wing backlash against the burgeoning welfare-state.

The fallacies inherent in the political approach are manifesting themselves in the Party by means of its rampant factionalism. Any group which attempts to gain mass support when there is no strong philosophical undercurrent will attract many undesirables, people who come into the group for social or emotional reasons. They come armed with little more than superficial understanding, and leave when they realize that their petty emotions will not or cannot be satisfied by the leadership. Or they try to take over.

Back to the 1975 convention, Rothbard reports that the Convention experienced a fierce resistance from what he calls a "Left Opposition." It seems that this "Left Opposition" wanted "kooky" candidates. Apparently, they believed that true libertarianism must be consistent and courageous enough to run candidates whose attitudes and activities are disapproved of by a majority of Americans. Their resistance to the "conservative" leadership indicates a strong desire to push the party into the advocacy of misguided and empty egalitarianism. Indeed, it seems that a putsch was attempted at the L.P. Convention back then.

An even more dangerous aspect of L.P. factionalism is shown through the Party's accommodation of anarchists. I quote again from Rothbard: "Finally, the famous minarchist vs. anarchocapitalist controversy is only dimly related to the struggle over the Left Opposition. Basically that controversy was happily settled at the Dallas convention in 1974 when it was decided that the L.P. platform should be purely libertarian, but that no stand should be taken one way or another on archy vs. anarchy thus fostering a coalition which both sides can live with.'

But is it such a happy coalition? Can both sides of this debate really work in harmony? What does libertarianism mean if both anarchists and limited government advocates see their goals differently? Let us see.

Anarchocapitalists and limited government advocates have two different political goals—the first to eliminate government, the second to establish a firmly limited government. If the L.P. does not take a stand on a proper government, then libertarian goals become obscure. Liberty becomes a word with double meanings, since it cannot mean the same to both sides. It cannot mean simply the absence of governmental coercion, since issues of political application are involved, issues that both sides see differently. Further, the issue of validating a proper societal order is seen differently by each side. Yet, these very issues require a great deal of clarity if the Party is to be a real alternative. Because of the coalition of limited government advocates and anarchists, Libertarianism would mean different things to different people and would force spokespeople into double-talk when they enter the political arena. Such compromises are more than political, they are philosophical.

In fact, the power struggle that was supposedly avoided by the '74 agreement served to give the anarchocapitalists control of the party. At a dinner on March 24, 1976, I asked Roger MacBride, the L. P. Presidential candidate for 1976, how he stood on this debate. He answered that we are not now in a position where such a debate is important, that what we need to do is turn things around in the direction of freedom. This may not seem like such a bad answer, but one must wonder at the implications of it with my next question. I asked

Mr. MacBride what his position on this debate would be if it ever became a major political issue. He answered that he would not be able to anticipate that. The obvious question was: Who pulls the strings in a party that prides itself as a Party of principle, and yet, whose Presidential candidate cannot take a stand on an issue of principle? The men in this Party's smoke-filled room are anarchists.

Were the L. P. truly a party of principle, I would never have gotten this kind of answer. No party has a chance of turning anything around if the dominant force in it, a force whose views are unpopular and predominantly unheard of, as well as wrong, exerts this kind of influence. I visualized a toy jack-in-the-box, marked "Libertarian Party" and with MacBride's picture on the outside, just brought home to a little boy who symbolizes the American voter. His face lights up as he winds the toy and listens to the music (vague slogans about liberty and unity). The shock comes when out of the box suddenly pops Murray Rothbard with a copy of "Power and Market". The surprise would make anyone cry and be afraid. The deception would be abhorrent.

Fortunately, the American voter is not a child, and he would be able to see through the façade of unity. The libertarians are fooling no one but themselves if they think they can educate through evasion.

Who is the actual winner in this factional debate that no one engages in? No one. The anarchists will never receive the respectability they are trying to steal by their advocacy of capitalism, and the limited government advocates will lose by associating themselves with anarchists. The voter? "Hog wash".

Those limited government advocates in the Party are supporting the Party which refuses to defend the proper form of government. It is not in their interests to promote spokespeople for libertarianism who, when asked about their political principles, base their answers on Rothbardian definitions and interpretations of history, all of which make no effort to justify limited government. In fact, the coalition creates a situation wherein limited government advocates must avoid bringing up speculation on how limited government would handle certain matters, while the anarchists are free to imply their positions by openly discussing the failures of government.

A Party of principle can never be achieved through power politics. What is needed is people of principle, and for this we need a great deal more work in the field of education. Education is the balance on the scale between a free society and tyranny. Reason is the measure that can tip the scale in favor of liberty. Vigilance is the weight that secures liberty.

A loose political coalition for the pursuit of liberty is merely an outgrowth of the pragmatism that must be debated and eliminated in our society by educators and leaders. When pragmatism is no longer an accepted political philosophy, then it will be time for a Party of principle. Until then, we must lay the philosophical foundations in metaphysics, epistemology and ethics to as wide an audience as possible. Almost none of this is happening today. (See my books "How Pragmatism Destroyed a World" and "Pragmatism on Display")

To focus vaguely on political goals is to evade the basic and more important issues without which political goals are impossible. These are metaphysical and epistemological in nature. It is expedient that we take time to develop clear and irrefutable philosophical arguments for liberty while the government's gun is still protecting our right to do so. By convincing enough people, we may be able to prevent its turning against us.

I am sure I will be accused of quibbling. To this I can only reply that compromise on the proper form of government will only ensure that it will never be achieved. Fundamental debates cannot be brushed aside until some future time. They must be discussed now. Anyone who is pretentious enough to posture as a defender of liberty while at the same time asking people to forget the basic arguments for liberty is asking for too much. I would not trust the man who does not quibble about man's rights. The last men who did so were the Founding Fathers.

To those who feel a desperate need to do something about our political situation, I would suggest this: Do everything you can to create a new mood in the two major political parties. It does not take that many people to create a vocal constituency. Politicians multiply opinions. Speak out for your rights to those who can more directly affect them. But more importantly, recognize that the real battle is in our educational institutions and, as parents, teachers, and college professors, we should do everything possible to create a new philosophical atmosphere. The real struggle for freedom is in the schools – and today, the progressives rule the day.

Indeed, the schools today are turning out little monster community organizers and social agitators who seek only to foment hatred of capitalism and individual initiative. Children who are not thought how to think are today being taught politics, how to appeal to and compromise with the grand collectives that they are taught to worship. Changing this horrendous environment and returning education to the purpose of teaching children how to think will take a monumental effort that must start with the parents.

I want to be clear here; I am not talking about trying to make conservativism into the correct philosophy. Conservatism is not based upon reason but upon faith; and specifically, faith, hope, and charity are not going to be the foundations that will establish individual liberty and individual rights. A new philosophy founded upon reason and the scientific process must be created. Men must see that integrating their correct observations of reality into a coherent new philosophical system is the only approach possible to the creation of a proper society.

What is Government?

In order to understand what government is and what it is supposed to do, we should understand the difference between a state and a limited government.

State

A state is the dominant institution in any territorial area that engages in both defensive and offensive activities with regard to those in its area. Its basic premise is that it owns all within its domain and can rightfully impose its will upon all.

From the philosophical arena, the advocates of statism hold (or imply) that the political system is responsible for implementing all the ethical decisions that its leaders choose. Statism requires the belief that man has no effective self-control regarding ethical matters, and that it is proper for the initiation of force against citizens to make them do as the state demands.

Limited Government

A limited government is an organization operating in a given territorial area whose purpose is to organize the instruments of force to defend the individual rights of those citizens who do not deny individual rights to others.

The relationship between politics and ethics in a limited government is the idea that man has free will and that his survival requires the exercise of reason. Society and cooperation were devised to further the interests of those men who chose to exercise their rational faculties, i.e., seek survival through peaceful, productive means.

Limited government was devised to control and fight those men who seek survival through force or fraud. But since volition applies to men in government as well, it is necessary to discourage irrational elements from achieving any short-term advantage from improper use of government.

A limited government accomplishes essentially two things: I) It protects the individual rights of the citizen, and 2) It provides a framework of legal impediments to make the corruption of governmental power impossible within the lifetime of any potential despot.

Non-coercive activities, in society, are, properly, not under the jurisdiction of a limited government. The government is expressly designed to enable morality in all areas except initiated force (by the individual or the government). It is not a vehicle for the imposition of morality over helpless victims, but is itself limited by morality.

By living within a government's territory, an individual implies his sanction of the government's laws, or a willingness to obey those laws he disapproves, under the conviction that through the political process he can change them. Because of the constitution, this sanction becomes a written contract of a sort. One signs it merely by being present and participating in society.

Proper legal compulsion is acquired in a limited government only after a clearly defined procedure is established, one which recognizes a citizen's rights and his possible innocence when charged. A legal system of objective laws integrated with the constitution sets the limits to what the government can do and how it should do it.

The foregoing discussion of statism and limited government reveals a clear distinction between the two. The only function they have in common is monopoly on defense services. Yet, this does not make them the same type of government. Limited government means "limited to defense"; statism means "unlimited rule." The anarchocapitalist position that limited government is a form of statism is totally false.

By arguing against a "state," and by unjustifiably categorizing limited government as a state, the anarchocapitalists allow themselves some major and convenient evasions. But the evasions include even their definition of anarchy. Rothbard writes: "On the other hand, I define anarchist society as one where there is no legal possibility for coercive aggression against the person or property of any individual."

Rothbard's definition of anarchy is merely semantics. There is no legal possibility for coercive aggression in anarchy because there is no possibility for legality. In anarchy, nothing could be legally considered to be coercive aggression. Likewise, individual rights would also have no legal foundation since there is no government agency to protect individuals except competing agencies at war with each other.

Anarchocapitalist writings frequently mention how man's rights might be protected by free market functions, in total neglect of the fact that man's rights cannot be consistently defended without documented approval of the citizenry, an approval which gives rise to the possibility of legality and objective law. Rights, although derived from the nature of man, cannot be achieved politically without a constitutional statement of them and a singular government's authority to uphold them. It is only limited government that can consistently ban coercion.

Since anarchy supplies no consistent implementation of man's rights in the legal sense, man's rights would remain at best a loose ideal in anarchy. Man's rights would be anyone's guess or opinion. The development of a legal system, in anarchy, would tend to be rudimentary and disintegrated. Anti-rights groups, in their competition with pro-rights groups, would have an interest in creating as much confusion as possible on issues of man's rights. There is every possibility that competing agencies will tend toward coercive activities in order to benefit clients. The danger of statism, therefore, looms ever-larger.

In fact, coercive aggression is very possible in anarchy. We can see how it is possible if we analyze the difference between production and force.

Production is a requirement of man's survival whether he lives in society or in nature. In fact, production reaches maximum benefit only in a social situation, because trade, division of labor and specialization then come about.

Force, however, achieves only destruction unless it is used to protect an innocent person against attack or fraud. It is anti-social in nature unless it is harnessed to protect those who go about the business of producing and trading. In this context, we find the division between initiated force and defense. Obviously, initiated force has no place in the market, since it disrupts and destroys productivity and trade. Defensive force, on the other hand, serves the purpose of combatting, deterring, and defeating those who initiate force.

Production and force are two opposites that cannot operate according to the same social laws. Production must be left alone. Force must be controlled and regulated by responsible citizens.

The market involves thousands of individual transactions, each dependent upon each man's reasoning capacity. Thousands of wrong decisions are made every day. But these only involve issues of production and trade, and the loss is to those who make the wrong choices. Because of the cumulative nature of capital and technology, the free market advances the general wellbeing nonetheless.

But if force is not banned from the market, a strong competition between rational and irrational elements is created, thereby effectively beating down the accumulation of capital and technology. Force is destructive, not productive. To take a loss on an issue of production is one thing, but the issue of force represents an entirely different ballgame.

If force without government (as in anarchocapitalism) were to go on the market, those elements that cannot compete successfully in the productive arena would receive a tremendous advantage. Their errors of judgment in productive matters could be easily made-up-for by the use of force. This means that coercion will compete openly with defense. In such a situation those men who would use force would have the advantage of ambush, theft, sabotage, bribery, blackmail, fraud, and murder.

On the other hand, the free market with force effectively banned by government has no provision for the coercive advancement of inferior products or services. They fall to better competition. In anarchy, they need not fall. And the effect of using force as a "bargaining tool," would be the diversion from production toward protection— constant warfare.

The free market depends for its success upon a well-defined, well instituted government. It cannot exist without one. Anarchocapitalists glorify the safety and security of a free market which allows for long-range action, totally evading the fact that, without a limited government, long-range action would deteriorate to the level of gun-slinging.

Without a proper view of man's survival, the political system that any given theorist might advocate would necessarily suffer from a lack of integration. The system, if implemented, would produce opportunities for flagrant activities on the part of evil men, since the theorist could not foresee the contradictions in his speculations. For instance, statism is based on the proposition that man is impotent in the face of moral decisions, and that he requires a political system to impose decisions upon him. This false view creates a situation through which plundering dictators achieve full control.

Limited government, on the other hand, institutes the idea that man's survival requires the exercise of reason in all matters of production and trade. This gives rise to a government that would defend his rights against those who would deny them.

The anarchist view holds that man's moral status is evil, weak, and manipulable. They ignore the fact that governments are not entities as such; they are comprised of men acting together. They act institutionally only in accordance with the views and attitudes of men. If all governments are coercive by nature, then all men must be prone to coercion. They must be evil by nature. The anarchists cannot possibly reconcile this form of composition with their professed view of man as a being of volition. Theirs is a collectivized view that declares all men incapable of making the right decisions and suggests that we leave those decisions up to the laws of the marketplace which somehow function as if they were a Hegelian (natural) construct.

Volition applies only to individual men. It reflects the basic ability of each man to make the decisions that life requires. Each man can choose to think or not to think. Volition only identifies the options for man in using his mind. It is this basic fact that gives rise to the necessity of a government. And it is this fact that makes anarchy an anti-human and inapplicable concept.

It is in the nature of political institutions in society that determines the relationship between good and evil. Volition, then, implies that a group of men can construct an effective government. But it does not imply that it will remain effective. Through time, men may lose their vigilance. To prevent against this, they need effective separations of power, effective representational systems and checks and balances. They also need constitutional expressions of rights that will serve to guide the courts in their dispensation of justice.

Man's volitional nature implies that an unprotected market can and must descend to the level where force is the ruling element. But it does not imply that the market will naturally become free of force. Volition holds no power in political institutions except that power that is reflected through vigilance. Anarchy, then, promises constant warfare.

On the other hand, limited government, provides a consistent and uniform barrier against force. It adds another dimension and a stronger measure of security to the concept of self-defense. This is because limited government allows the individual to deal with self-defense only on the intellectual level of the organization of his government, rather than on the brute physical level. This releases him to do the job of advancing his wellbeing by concentrating on production and trade.

Without a limited government, a free market on force would work predominantly to the interest of evil. Look at the bloody history of this planet for an indication of which way man's societies have gone without proper limits on forceful activities. Contrary to the anarchist belief, the history of the world does not prove that governments are evil by nature, but that improper control of force can have catastrophic results.

If anarchocapitalists want to fight for a government-less society, they would be more honest if they mimicked the Sophists of ancient times proclaiming that might should be right. It is because anarchy is basically an anti-rights concept that anarchocapitalist advocacy of capitalism amounts to nothing more than lip-service. The anarchocapitalists are de facto enemies of capitalism, and so is the Libertarian Party that advocates anarchocapitalism.

Rothbard: "If a man's free will to adopt ideas and values is inalienable, his freedom of action - his freedom to put these ideas into effect in the world - is not in such a fortunate condition."[9] So much for Rothbard's assessment of free will.

Let's make no mistake about this: the professed belief in volition stressed by anarchocapitalists merely represents window-dressing. Their actual premise is that all governments are evil. In any period of history, an anarchist can don any philosophical coat. But whether he acknowledges it or not, the principle he has always fought for is "might makes right."

The history of the development of limited government shows a progression toward more control over the government, with a consequent progression toward more individual freedom. The framers of these systems were intent upon eliminating the power that governments and rulers could wield over people. Each experiment succeeded somewhat, but each also realized flaws that allowed despotic types the opportunity to take advantage of constitutional loopholes.

---

[9] http://www.brainyquote.com/quotes/authors/m/murray_rothbard.html

The record does not reveal that governments are evil by nature, but that statism (which has infiltrated limited government) is evil by nature. A continuing effort to perfect limited government is in order. It would be unwise to forsake a chance for a true liberty by compromising with or even giving the benefit of the doubt to those who favor a system from which any form of despotism lies just a premise or a gun away.

What is a proper society?

History has shown us many great civilizations. The Hittites, the Aegean people, the Romans and the Greeks, to name a few, constructed impressive cultures of tremendous power and reach. Their achievements are the recorded legacies that have filtered down to our civilization and have provided some of the most fundamental aspects of our lives. Our ability to integrate the better aspects of past civilizations has helped in making ours the greatest civilization in mankind's history.

Yet, for centuries, at least during recorded history, many of these civilizations were nominally based upon plunder and domination. And, it was during early, recorded history (and possibly before) that men experimented with various forms of government in order to curtail the encroachments of bloody, looting tyrants bent on domination, slavery and tribute. Among such tyrants, concepts like individual rights were unknown. I submit that today the situation is much the same as during ancient times and that many of the worst aspects of plundering dictatorships are playing out today.

Barbarism is a negative, an absence of knowledge and institutional control. Its best representatives have characterized their reigns by plunder, murder, and rape. They leave only destruction and decline in their passing. Their social components leave no enduring features because there is little worth preserving. The history from which we are supposed to learn is the history of barbarism, the history of Darius, Attila, and Hitler, the history that says if you "rule" over men, you can take what you want and do what you want.

The civilized man does not want to be ruled. He is characterized by a respect for the rights of others, by a dedication to long-range values, by productiveness and rationality. He is a man who can be counted upon to seek and do those things that benefit him and harm no others. He is a man who knows that good results proceed from honesty in his dealings with other men. The difference between a civilized man and a barbarian is that when a civilized man sees a defenseless woman wearing a diamond ring, he compliments her on its beauty. When the barbarian sees her, he knocks her over the head and takes it.

The civilized man and the barbarian are two opposites with two different philosophies, and their civilizations are expressions of the way they see the world, and of the values they seek. The civilized man is educated and uses abstract, validated knowledge, while the barbarian operates upon concrete-bound thinking, whim, and prejudiced un-validated notions. The civilized man thinks, the barbarian reacts to the pit of his stomach. To the barbarian, the civilized man exists to give up his loot. To the civilized man, the barbarian must be eliminated in order that men are able to survive beyond the next minute.

One issue that is little understood today, and much less discussed, is the theory relating to why men join society. This may seem like a strange way to frame the question, but in effect, each man does make a decision, once he understands the nature of the particular society into which he is born, to either accept its precepts or reject them. And indeed, it is the responsibility of every man to understand the fundamental factors that make up his/her society. Various statements are heard in contemporary literature naming the division of labor and the benefits derived from it as the major reasons for society; but little is heard concerning man's means of survival, and how this relates to an organized society.

Since some men choose to think, and thereby survive by the use of their minds, and other men choose not to think, a society cannot provide any benefits unless it protects the exercise of the rational faculty by those who choose to exercise it. This is done through the recognition of the fact that nature does not provide man's sustenance automatically, but that it must be achieved intellectually. Those aspects of reality upon which a man exercises his rational faculty necessarily become his property—not available to any other man except by voluntary exchange. By protecting property, government protects the right of a man to his life, and thereby makes a happy and successful life possible.

Freedom (liberty) can only be established after the creation of an intellectual framework of ideas that are rooted in reality. Men act in reality, but their rights only exist if other men honor them, recognize them, and understand them. Rights do not come from nature or the free market; they come from man's mind as it observes reality.

Limited government is not statism, but the only system in history devised to replace it. The central focus of limited government is man's volitional nature, and its purpose is to protect man's right to make his own decisions and rational actions. Only on this basis can a clear understanding of limited government be obtained.

Man is a creature that survives by means of his mind, especially by his ability to learn and use knowledge to determine correct action. A valid society is one that allows intellectual freedom to function. It does this by protecting each man in the pursuit of life, happiness, and survival. If it does not protect this, if instead it thwarts man's efforts, it is not a valid society and it would be better for man to live in primitive nature. There can be no more important issue than whether society protects man's fundamental rights or violates them.

One of the first known discussions about proper social organization came when the ancient Persians were trying to decide the kind of government they would have. They debated on whether they should have a democracy, an oligarchy, or a monarchy. The men who fostered each type of government spoke and gave their best arguments for their favorite system. Darius (521-486 B.C.), the eventual despot, spoke in favor of a monarchy. He proclaimed that power when in the hands of one man could more effectively be exerted in favor of the people. The issue was decided, not by vote or agreement among the leading citizens, but by the neighing of a horse (which should make one wonder how serious were these "founding fathers").

Mankind decides few things in this fashion today, particularly issues of such monumental importance as the kind of government they should adopt. Deliberation over such issues should be done with extreme caution and long debate to guard against the development and growth of tyranny. The slightest philosophical mistake leaves the door to destruction open. Indeed, the idea of "constituted" government must have developed in the ancient world because of the despotism and cruelty of men like Darius.

Yet, if we closely examine the work of Herodotus, the historian who told this story about the Persian "Constitutional Convention," one will notice that there seemed to be an undercurrent to the events surrounding the rise of Darius. That undercurrent reveals the existence of a debate about proper government during that time. The undercurrent reveals that honest, productive men wanted to be free of despots and tyrants; they sought to be protected against plunder and servitude. I believe that this struggle of honest men to protect themselves against violation is the underlying purpose of all discussions of proper government. Men yearned to be protected against the encroachment of those who would rather take, at the point of a sword, what had been created by honest labor. In other words, honest men need to be protected against, not only the dishonest among them, but against the tyranny of those who would presume to organize society as a means to the fulfillment of their self-serving goals. Men need to be protected against out-of-control government.

As men congregated into small agricultural communities, they built the foundations for advanced civilizations. The division of labor, the invention of money and other advances served to create societies that were worth preserving. In order to handle marauders and thieves, they created law courts and wrote down their laws on stone in order to create a long-lasting civil society. Yet, as soon as these inventions were brought to the fore, there arose men who sought to "rule" rather than legislate. Some of these men took over the courts and legislative bodies and strove to create "protection rackets" that enabled them to protect peaceful citizens while at the same time engaging in schemes to steal their abundance. The "state" developed while leaders walked a fine line between protection, theft, and territorial expansion. Productive men needed protection, but they did not need legislated morality or conquest. They needed civility, trade, civil rights, and property. They needed liberty.

A society is defined by its institutions. These are given life by the ideas they embody. Ideas give form and order to a society if they are proper, and they give chaos and decline if they are impractical. This has been proven many times over. The extent to which a civilization's ideas are advanced and correct is the extent of the greatness of that civilization. The extent to which its ideas are false and inapplicable is the extent to which it is barbaric or in decline. To understand this further, let us look at how Darius defended the idea of monarchy. Herodotus puts the words into his mouth.

"...if three forms are proposed, and each of these which I allude to the best in its kind, the best democracy, and oligarchy, and monarchy, I affirm that the last is far superior; for nothing can be found better than one man, who is the best; since acting upon equally wise plans, he would govern the people without blame, and would keep his designs most secret from the ill-affected. But in an oligarchy, while many are exerting their energies for the public good, strong private enmities commonly spring up; for each wishing to be chief, and to carry his own opinions, they come to deep animosities one against another, from whence seditions arise; and from seditions, murder; and from murder it results in anarchy; and thus it is proved how much this form of government is the best. But when the people rule, it is impossible but that evil should spring up; when, therefore, evil springs up, mutual enmities do not arise among the bad, but powerful combinations, for they who injure the commonwealth act in concert; puts them down; and on this account he is admired by the people, and being admired, he becomes a monarch; and in this he too shows that a monarchy is best. But to comprehend all in one word, whence came our freedom? and who gave it? Was it from the people, or an oligarchy, or a monarch? My opinion, therefore, is, that if we were made free by one man, we should maintain the same kind of government; and, moreover, that we should not subvert the institutions of our ancestors, seeing they are good; for that were not well."[10]

Darius, of course, had himself in mind for the monarchy and the freedom he praised was the freedom to be ruled (or protected) by him. His views won the day with a little help from treachery and deceit. The idea then that only one man can govern effectively is the basic premise upon which all tyrannies are justified (See Hitler). All other men are to be mere subjects who are allotted the task of providing the all-knowing monarch with the fulfillment of his "secrets" (whims).

The idea that a particular king or dictator would be the best to rule a nation has been eloquently disproved by history countless times. Indeed, the idea that "the best" kind of man would somehow become king is patently false especially in situations where "the best" are not allowed to come to power due to "low" birth or privilege. I submit that if "the best" of men were to somehow rise to prominence in a monarchy, the most valuable thing he could do for his "subjects" is to establish their individual rights; to free them from the yoke of a system where "the king's

---

[10] Herodotus, The History, Thallia. III, 83

prerogative" or the guild is the only way to succeed. He would abolish his own power and protect freedom.

Darius believed that tyranny must inevitably be the foundation of every society. In his view, either the tyrant rules over others or "the people" (who do not possess the knowledge or training) rule haphazardly. The idea of a society where no man has the right to "rule" others had not occurred to him and probably had occurred to few other men of that time. Perhaps this is the "knowledge" that a man bent on kingship and power cannot allow into his consciousness. Since those times, we have learned that the principle of individual rights is the very principle that releases men from the whims of the mob and/or the king. And, indeed, the rule of the mob or the rule of the tyrant are abolished in proper societies.

Because men are fallible (including kings and dictators), the consequences of institutionalizing one-man rule have always been decline and destruction. The barbarism that results from monarchy fills the history books; benevolent monarchs notwithstanding. It took millennia of philosophical development before men could devise a government like that in the United States of America where the idea was to protect the individual from power, plunder, and governmental misuse. That development resulted in a government of limited functions where people could live their lives without fear of expropriation of their property. This idea, a constitutionally limited government, had the intent of making it possible for men to live in a civilized fashion.

Although much of ancient literature glorifies tyrants, there were some thinkers, like Aristotle, who wrote about the concept of constitutional government. Later, as Christianity advanced, the idea of a constitutionally limited government became lost. Mankind floated on the legacy of an ancient religion that had little regard for civility and prosperity. The governments of various Christian sects were bent more toward humility, faith, obedience, and worship. Men were instructed to live with heads bowed and eyes down in keeping with piety. To make sure this happened, a caste system developed that created harmony between church and state. The Dark Ages and their cruelties were the result.

During these times, men educated solely by the Church began to believe some bizarre things. They believed in alchemists who searched for the philosopher's stone, a chemical that could help turn metals into gold. Potentates and kings and bishops, all over Europe spent inordinate amounts of wealth keeping alchemists busy in their experiments. These men devised various means for fooling the rich and the gullible by claiming to cure diseases with magnets and other "medicines", amassing huge fortunes in the process. The numerous witch trials fostered by potentates such as England's King James routinely sent hundreds of thousands of people to the pyre on no evidence whatsoever. Again, other church-sponsored charlatans developed bizarre tortures intended to "prove" that totally innocent people were guilty of collaborating with the devil. These charlatans also became quite wealthy inventing various methods such as driving pins into the bodies of people to detect if they had the mark of Satan upon them or wrapping people in blankets to see if they would drown or float. The drowned died (meaning they were innocent) were released, and those who floated were killed as witches. In many cases, all it took were the accusations of children (some of whom had playfully swallowed pins) to have someone burned at the stake. I find it strange that few people at the time realized that the people killed as witches were being sent to the very place where their mentor (Satan) resided. No one realized that killing them was hardly a punishment.

Needless to say, the follies and idiocies that rose up during these times were all part of the Christian heritage, part and parcel to the beliefs in ghosts, demons, spirits and god's minions. The intellectual state of these people was abysmal and yet few people blamed the church for all of these thousands upon thousands of atrocities inflicted on innocent people. Add to that the unscientific view of knowledge and the persecutions of people like Galileo, Giordano Bruno and others and you can see that the essence of rationalism is the Christian mind.

These Dark Ages persisted until the re-discovery of ancient philosophy and art. When this occurred, the ideas of the ancient world about constitutionally limited governments re-surfaced and the idea of man as thinker and freethinker began to develop. Europe became awash with new ideas, men of independent minds began to question the status quo and challenge the excesses of the ruling classes. Logic and the scientific method made a resurgence and man began once again to learn about nature and the world. The advance of technology resumed, and new forms of social organization developed that permitted talented and skilled people to function without fear.

Eventually, the Magna Carta restricted the power of Britain's rulers and constitutional governments were again the subject of discussion. Throughout this period, the power of the Church loomed ever so large. Its ideas and its hold on the mind of man continued and many intelligent men became confused about their loyalties. Having a questioning mind was a sin against God.

And yet, many Christians continued to believe in their religion and in many of its precepts. This created a philosophical contradiction that led to a split between secular philosophers who pursued truth outside the confines of religion, and theologians who interpreted the world from the precepts of rationalism, miracles, fantasies, and paradoxes. This split, because the Church was so powerful, led to the acceptance of many Christian precepts. In particular, moral dualism, a chief Christian precept went unchallenged.

But man is not guilty or impotent by nature. Volition is the singular most essential aspect of man, for in it is contained the basic difference between man and animals. Volition relates to one choice: to think or not to think[11] which means that the choice for every man is either to gain knowledge and survive or to remain ignorant and fail. The choice an individual makes on this issue determines, more than any other issue, the direction his life will take.

It takes a complete and consistent philosophy to help a man advance from the first step, which is that decision to think. It takes an understanding of the way reason and knowledge operate in a man's consciousness to take the next step. It takes a singular purpose, a goal, in order for a man to benefit from his knowledge gained. It takes a further advance to the discovery of the virtues and rights that proceed from a recognition of the value of man's mind, and it takes a further advance to respect individual rights in one's personal life and in government.

When men look around to society looking for a way to ensure freedom and protection, they learn that the first principle is to leave people free and not assault their rights. The individual is the first

[11] Ayn Rand should be credited with first making this point.

person who can secure his own freedom by leaving other men free. He would also countenance other people in his society to understand that this "first principle" is the key to social living.

As he continues to understand how free societies should work, he notices that some people are not interested in respecting the rights of others; some are more interested in reversing cause and effect to obtain the products created through freedom without actually being productive themselves. They would just as soon bash people over the head and take their possessions. What would the honest man do in such a situation? He would notice that his society works best when men divide their labors and cooperate to create products, and to trade with one another. He would look for someone who would develop a specialty in protection and hire him to protect his rights within the framework of a limited government. He would also be joined in this by others who want to be protected. As long as *this* "policeman" served all people fairly, it would be possible to have a "government" that only protected people.

It is important to understand the uniqueness of these concepts of freedom and limited government. What it requires is the recognition that morality is not about sacrificing goods but about keeping those goods and privately disposing of them according to self-interest. This new approach, the way of freedom, represents an innovation both in terms of morality but also in terms of the way society is constructed.

Property rights do not derive from the conservative position that all men are different and would do differently with similar types of property. They derive from the fact that each man survives by production and that he must be free both to own his property and to dispose of the products of his labor. Otherwise, he has no incentive to produce—he will not produce if he must appease looting thugs or bureaucrats. Property rights derive from man's productive nature; and since production is an ethical, moral requirement of life, property rights are the most fundamental ethical principle in political theory. Because property rights are a fundamental principle, they must become the base upon which all other principles of society and government depend. No violation of property rights is moral-- no justification is more important, no argument more just, than the idea that property rights must be recognized above all other claims. Property rights are the cornerstone of individual rights.

To clarify the issue of property rights let us examine the function of one of society's most vital institutions, the contract. A contract is a written, legally protected agreement between two or more participants, undertaken voluntarily, for the purpose of trading goods or services held by the parties as their property. In short, a contract is an exchange of property undertaken for the sake of the long-range benefits of all trading parties. Should any participant default on his part of a contract he would violate the contract and deprive the other participants of the property or service he or she agreed to exchange. Were the contract not protected by government, were someone allowed to get away with defaulting, then the property rights of the others would not be protected. When property rights are denied on a global scale, society disintegrates, and the long-range benefits of society would disappear. The dictator, shyster, and altruist would be the heroes of the day. The productive man would be stifled and undercut.

Why does man join society? Because his life is immeasurably improved when his right to property (his right to pursue happiness) is protected.

Property cannot be protected in the wild except by constant struggle and violence against thieves and wild animals. Long-range action and planning become possible when a person fears no living man or the arbitrariness of a government official. Only then can we exploit the benefits of the division of labor, capital accumulation and technology. A safe, secure, happy life is only possible to a productive man.

When a society is ruled by laws that violate the right to property (as our society today does), then the safety and security found in society disappear and there is no reason to participate in it (except that one decides to struggle to make it free). It is as if the jungle had reclaimed the intellectual infrastructure of the society. In such a society, a man knows not whom to fear so he fears all. His actions become short-range because a thief, heavy taxation, inflation, or new government regulations threaten his future production. And slowly, the only property defended by government is government property.

The government should be, properly, a limited agency; limited to the defense of property rights. When such a government is achieved, society can then function for the self-interest of those willing to survive honestly and to the detriment of those who seek parasitism. The closest mankind has come to establishing a perfect society was after the American Revolution. The Constitution of the United States established a government limited to the defense of the rights (only) of those citizens who chose to survive by means of reason. It was a system of government with some imperfections, and indeed the Founding Fathers did not fully realize the scope of what they were accomplishing, but it can be said that they fully understood the importance of limiting the actions of men who might use government for coercive intent.

The idea of a government limited to protecting inalienable rights is such a new idea historically that few have scarcely grasped it even 240 plus years after the U.S. Constitution was inaugurated. Yet, it is this concept of government, more than any other that has provided the opportunity for a truly good and virtuous man to exist in harmony with other men. The most dangerous threat to this system is the altruist morality. It is this morality, in its various forms, that is responsible for the moral inversion that views self-interest as an evil concept. It is altruism, enacted into law, that will eventually turn our society to the dark side. We are seeing this ever so eloquently today in the utter banality of our political processes.

Establishing Freedom in Society

An intellectual atmosphere for political freedom is an abstraction that many people do not understand because:

   l) we do not have such an atmosphere today, and

   2) it is difficult to see how it would operate.

Imagine a situation in which a great many influential people understand the metaphysical and epistemological bases for man's rights, wherein most educators are able to prove that man has rights and are teaching the principles of a proper society to a great many young people.

These educators and young people, being of large enough numbers, would then have an effect upon the printed and visual media, the arts, and upon politics. Political constituencies would develop that demanded politicians should do the job of protecting the individual against the encroachment of his rights. In fact, the politician would be required to agree with the concept of man's rights before he could be elected. The debates and issues in such a situation would be clear. The entire society would stand vigilant watch against the beginnings of tyranny.

More than this, the people, well-educated and well-versed in the language of liberty, would demand that no government official of any type be able to rightfully declare coercive laws and regulations against any citizen or group of citizens. These people would demand that their government be constituted in such a way that government only protects individual rights.

Certainly, the establishment of such an atmosphere requires a gradual, long-range view among those people engaged in promoting political freedom. This long-range view, however, must have a beginning in the metaphysical and epistemological principles that form the foundation for the ethical principles that inform the constitution of a proper society. Along the way, many positive signs may be seen as society becomes the protector of rights and not the violator of them.

When people would start demanding that rights not be sacrosanct, that they should instead submit to the whims of treacherous people eager to steal their value, it would be easy for teachers to correct false views and put society back on track by using objective knowledge and reason. Tyranny would not be able to overcome people who understand and love their freedoms.

But until that atmosphere is established, there can be no compromise with those who lean toward freedom but whose activities or ideas jeopardize the movement. We must avoid common cause with people who smuggle an anti-rights perspective in the name of individual rights. This would include the various anarchists and leftists of whatever variety. People would recognize that there can be, nor should there be, any compromise with people who seek to undermine freedom and elevate force in society.

Since anarchism, as an apolitical concept, allows no compromise, the intent and goals of anarchists must be to propagandize against limited government. Anarchists will do all they can to establish their own intellectual atmosphere which would put them at odds with those who advocate limited government. This is why it is important that observant intellectuals understand the true goals and methods of those who would undermine freedom. Anyone who would argue against individual rights is necessarily an enemy of freedom. The fantasy that anarchy can defend individual rights must be exposed.

Short-sighted goals and misguided activities (such as the Libertarian Party) appeal to people only if they drop the context of the long-range goal. That the promoters of such goals and activities use the rhetoric of liberty does not mean that their understanding of liberty is correct.

Along the way toward a philosophical atmosphere that defends individual rights, there will be many profiteers, many who want to promote the impression that they were first or ahead of their time. Many will be conspicuous in the manner in which they try to exploit the suspicious trend toward tyranny. Others will be more deceptive. Still others will be sincere but misguided. The danger is that these people will mislead.

It is essential that all defenders of man's rights be viewed with the closest scrutiny. A statist is easy to identify. It is those who agree with us that we must challenge as much, if not more, than the statist. Our worst enemy, moral compromise, may be within, clothed in a subtle array of ambiguities, double meanings, and unstated premises. We owe it to ourselves to be vigilant.

For the same reason that an advocate of limited government should never compromise with an advocate of interventionism, an advocate of limited government should never compromise with an advocate of anarchy. Both interventionism and anarchy are opposed to limited government. Despite what interventionists may say, they want to do away with the concept of a controlled government and replace it with a system that gives oligarchs and government officials the ability to use force against honest citizens.

Consider the months of debate and discussion that surrounded the creation of the United States Constitution. That it was even created (with only a small amount of contradiction) can be attributed to the fact that there was considerable agreement on certain basic and necessary concepts. That it took months to draft this document indicates the degree of consensus which such issues held. To compromise now on these issues leaves us open to the same contradictions in a future Constitutional Convention, if it doesn't prevent our even having one.

Spreading the Right Ideas

The concept of political freedom arises only within the context of a limited government. Political freedom is the absence of governmental coercion. It requires a rigid governmental structure that has only one goal: the protection of the rights that proceed from man's means of survival. Political freedom pushes criminals outside the protection of government and places self-defense under the control of those who would foster the interests of productive and peaceful people. Political freedom makes an ethical and a social life possible.

Few governmental systems have been openly in favor of "man's means of survival". Few theorists have argued for defending such a concept. However, the de facto concept (which limited government is founded to protect) is "man's means of survival". Indeed, "man's rights" and "natural rights" have been the more common terms, and I have shown the fallacy of using the term "natural rights" above.

If one wants to achieve a value such as political freedom, one must know how best to achieve it, and how long it will take for its realization. In the realm of ideas, then, the key issue is how to disseminate ideas throughout the culture and that means education of the young. We can't be pure pragmatists about it and think we are going to influence adults who have already been educated. We must focus our efforts toward education of the young and preparing them to live as adults, rather than to focus education on a group of people who will not be convinced. The latter effort should be done through higher education and the media. Although the effort to educate adults can be part of the continuing dialogue among free people, the trend today for adults is away from educating for freedom.

Since the justification for teaching a life of liberty requires the identification of true reality, only consistent arguments (consistent with reality) will work. There are no shortcuts to the achievement of values, especially if those values are long-range, as is the concept of liberty. To attempt short-cuts (taking unwarranted bold leaps) is to drop the context and lose sight of the long-range goal. Any such short-cuts will fail.

The political approach of the Libertarian Party, that involves putting up candidates, is one of those short-cuts. The proper time for political campaigns is after progressives and conservatives have lost favor in the universities. When this happens, we will know that the culture is on the verge of transforming toward a new political paradigm. At that point, politicians will rise up as a natural outgrowth of the new cultural context. It will not be necessary to have a political approach since the right candidates will find their constituents.

Those who claim that we can't do anything about the trend toward statism are correct if we are talking about the present context. The best we can do today politically is to work within the established parties to insert a "stream of sanity" into the debates. This can have a limited impact because politicians will do what they think will earn votes and if there are vocal minorities in the parties, they can have a limited influence.

In my book, Crushing the Alinsky Radicals[12], I suggested that a new group rise up. This group would be dedicated specifically to advancing capitalism and its viability. This group (which I called the New Capitalist Radicals) would make the case to the American public that capitalism is the only system that advances and protects (through limited government), the rights of individuals to

---

[12] http://amzn.to/2daZCLp

live freely and make their own decisions. This group would also infiltrate the universities and challenge the hold progressives have there by advancing educators who provide valid (not necessarily conservative) arguments for liberty and capitalism.

Those who refuse to go through the effort of establishing a philosophical atmosphere, and resort, instead, to blind protests or activities, those who proclaim they want liberty now, like children stamping their feet at their parents' refusal to make their wishes come true, will meet with little support. Those who think they can make a jump straight from an out-of-context idea directly into political action cannot affect a positive future. No one should consider those children (in particular the libertarians and their anarchist fellow-travelers) to be ahead of their time.

If one is an educator, one should do all one can to improve his arguments for a proper society. Above all, he should not compromise to the extent of playing all sides of the philosophical fences (including pragmatism). There is no in-between in matters of this kind. There is no substitute (in prestige or result) for consistency. Further, the educator should not labor under the notion that the cause of liberty is lost. It is not lost, as long as he has the power to speak and teach. Ideas move a culture, and the educator is a man of ideas.

If one is not an educator, one should seek out those educators who are doing an adequate job and encourage them, promote them, quote them, and speak out on their views. One should try to spread what little philosophical influence there is on the subject of man's rights. One should write to one's congressman, and discuss the issues with him in terms of principle.

There are a great many ways through which one can spread the ideas of man's rights. The issues to expound upon are countless and growing every day as the government grows. But before one begins doing so, one should know clearly what one is talking about and why it is right. For this, I highly recommend the writings of Ayn Rand.

Today's Libertarian Party

The campaign of Gary Johnson added considerable strength to my contention that a Libertarian Party is an ineffective way to fight for liberty. As of this writing (October 2016) I have seen only one national campaign ad on television about his candidacy. Two points should be elaborated upon, and they should be viewed from the standpoint of the T. V. watcher and potential voter who is unfamiliar with libertarianism.

On domestic issues, the economy, balancing the budget, reducing the debt, etc., Johnson sounds much like a typical conservative. He says very little about rights and a separation of economics and government. He is essentially a conservative who praises free markets from a conservative base. How can he make much difference when we know that conservatives have approved virtually all of the big spending programs that liberals have fostered?

Another issue is Johnson's stand on foreign policy. The idea of eliminating all forms of U. S. foreign intervention reveals an amateurish (libertarian) understanding of international relations which most Americans would reject out of hand. It is known that Rothbard held similar notions and deemed them consistent with a global free market strategy. Since Rothbard decried government, Johnson's foreign policy (and that of Ron and Rand Paul) is consistent with the view that there should be no government influence in international affairs. There should be no foreign policy.

Before the U.S. can withdraw its 'intervention" in the affairs of other nations, it must first be assured that Soviet Russia and China would stop *their* interventions. Mr. Johnson's statements do not mention what he would do about Russian and Chinese intervention, an issue that is of prime concern for the American public; an omission that shows the inability of the Libertarian Party to effectively deal with international coercive movements and infiltration into American society.

It is from views of this type that we see a Presidential candidate who does not even know what Aleppo is. We have here an eloquent proof, on national television, of my contention that libertarians cannot argue for limited government but are free to imply anarchism. An anarchical system would not be able to respond to the actions of dictators and international killers while a limited government would have the ability and the responsibility to the security of its own citizens.

Johnson's position is based on the belief that the world naturally tends toward freedom without government (U.S.) involvement. This clearly shows that libertarians (and the anarchists who manipulate them) would unilaterally withdraw from the world under the false belief that the market would continue to function. But, as we have shown, free markets are an outgrowth of a philosophical premise that adheres to individual rights. In an anarchist scheme, any dictator can take over wherever he wants with no moral stand taken against them by the most powerful nation on earth. This is ludicrous.

In terms of current policy, the Libertarian Party does not stand for liberty, it stands for pragmatic politics and whim worship. A libertarian politics can only copy currently popular issues and is devoid of fundamental principles. How can a libertarian candidate advance liberty when he stands for a withdrawal from the world and an acceptance of the dictatorial movements that have decimated history?

Are we to assume that libertarianism means liberty? No. Are we to assume that libertarians fight for individual rights? No. Are we to assume that the ultimate goal is to create a free society? No. We cannot take anything for granted when it comes to the Libertarian political movement. Why should we? Johnson's candidacy provided no reason to believe that libertarians would fight for these things.

In summary, the principles of libertarianism are antithetical to the ideas of liberty and limited government. Libertarians falsely claim that all (possible) governments are statist and, as a result, they give over the world to the tyrants and dictators who would exploit and devastate humanity with their cruelties.

We can be certain that libertarians will take positions they consider anti-state. For instance, they could support fascist revolutions in various parts of the world while opposing Israel (as statist); they could refuse to oppose Russia and Communist China (as well as Iran) as those governments expand their territories and steal our patents.

Notice that libertarians will oppose liberation movements against tyranny (as state tyranny) but proclaim free trade with dictatorships such as Iran. Even nuclear proliferation would be considered by libertarians as supporting "the state"; by this view, nuclear weapons are illegitimate and have nothing to do with defending our liberties against tyrannical dictators who also have them. Libertarianism is a form of disarmament on a massive scale – except for the fact that the goal is for *us* to disarm not the Russians, Chinese, or Iranians.

In truth, libertarians will tell you that their quarrel is not with dictators and tyrants but with anything that represents the state. As such, their argument is with the U.S.A. They reflect the views of the anarchists among them, and this puts them at odds with the average American who would never coddle dictators. The way to fight dictatorship, they say, is to let the dictators create competing agencies of force.

Certainly, the party has changed over the years, but one thing is still evident: few libertarians advocate limited government as such. They continue to work within the framework of the existing election system but have seldom *voiced* the position of limited government. That goal of eliminating limited government remains a hidden agenda item for them. The pragmatists in the party are still in charge.

These four books by Robert Villegas comprise some of the business books that he has written. As an executive working for several companies, he was able to develop these methods that will help anyone seeking to excel in the business world. These books are:

How to Be a Great Employee – and a Greater Manager

You cannot be a great manager without first being a great employee. And this is something that requires learning, experience and attitude. The attitude comes from you but the learning and experience you should acquire through diligent study and practice. http://amzn.to/2BqdG2i $3.99 Kindle $8.95 softcover

SWOT Analysis Supercharged

A SWOT Analysis is an objective look at the internal and external elements of your organization that impact your success or lack thereof. If done diligently, you will always have a handle on what you need to do to improve season after season.
http://amzn.to/2BCAWYx $3.99 Kindle $6.95 softcover

The Five-Module Call Center Training System

The Five-Module Call Center Training System is designed to assist the Call Center Team Leader in helping his employees quickly upgrade their skills to an acceptable level. http://amzn.to/2B3Svj1 $3.99 Kindle $5.95 softcover

Website Development Methodology

Effective strategic marketing requires the ability to differentiate the website development organization and its deliverables from those of the competition. http://amzn.to/2DnYMqh $2.99 Kindle $12.95 softcover.

www.robertvillegas.com

Alcoholism and Addiction – the System

These four books comprise a system that can be used by both patients and counselors who are battling Alcoholism and Addiction. Based upon Mr. Villegas's own system developed during his struggle against alcoholism, this system includes:

Alcoholism and Addiction – A Secular Ten-Step Program

This groundbreaking book offers a secular approach to alcoholism unlike that offered by Alcoholics Anonymous. We recommend that every individual going for alcohol and drug-abuse counseling be given a copy of this book which contains the workbook and the two versions of The World's first drunk. http://amzn.to/2md6R9w $3.45 Kindle $11.95 softcover

The Secular Ten-Step Program Workbook

This booklet covers the program developed by Mr. Villegas. It is designed as a workbook with blank spaces for the patient to write his own thoughts as he takes each of the ten steps. Order one copy for each patient in counseling. http://amzn.to/2IrHimS $4.49 Kindle $6.95 softcover

The World's First Drunk – With Counselor Talking Points

This booklet is designed for the counselor as he works with patients during individual or group therapy. It contains helpful tips on discussing the life story of the man who invented alcohol. Order one copy for each patient in counseling. http://amzn.to/2I446Wr $2.99 Kindle $5.95 softcover

The World's First Drunk – Patient Version

This version of the short story contains empty spaces where the patient can answer questions about the life story of the man who invented alcohol. Order one copy for each counselor. http://amzn.to/2IdxBGb $2.99 Kindle $5.95 softcover.

www.robertvillegas.com

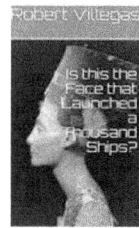

The Mark of Titus

Excerpts from the book Unkilling Jesus which highlight some of the key discoveries implied by new theories about the origin of the Jesus Myth. The idea that the Romans invented Christianity is the basic premise of new theories about the origin of Christianity.http://amzn.to/2itMCoO $3.49 Kindle $5.95 softcover

Contra Religion

This book is designed as a "shorter" explanation of the ideas presented in my larger book, "Behind the Ritual Mask" which seeks to define fundamental principles of religion. I'm hoping this book will serve as a primer for the original book and spur an interest in reading it. http://amzn.to/2yWMSlx $3.99 Kindle $6.95 softcover

Is this the Face that Launched a Thousand Ships?

It was love at first sight. I saw her one day while watching a television program about King Tut, whose tomb had been discovered by Howard Carter years before. I was looking at the famous bust of a beautiful Egyptian Queen. https://amzn.to/3t487x3 $3.99 Kindle $7.95 softcover

The History of Altruism

The History of Altruism is a historical treatment of the development of altruism throughout time from the Paleolithic period to today. It tracks the development of self-sacrifice of primitive man to the advent of altruism as a development from Kant's "duty". It covers a broad sweep of concepts and shows how they influenced modern man, religion and societies through the ages. https://amzn.to/3gN8zgy $4.19 Kindle 14.95 paperback.

www.robertvillegas.com

Unkilling Jesus

Who was Paul and what was his role in the creation of Christianity? What was his provenance, and did he meet the resurrected Christ? Who wrote Revelation and what was the document's purpose? Why was Domitian assassinated? http://amzn.to/2itMCo0 $3.99 Kindle $15.95 softcover

Domitian: The Final Messiah

The central goal of this book is to define the specific themes and concepts that make up Domitian's contribution to Christianity – in a sense, we are defining the specific Domitian overlay to the Christian materials originally developed for Titus. http://amzn.to/2yWMSlx $2.99 Kindle $6.95 softcover

Paul's Agon and the Mystification of History

Paul and Jesus are joined in one important way; the way of a miracle. They met on the road to Damascus while Paul supposedly pursued Christians. Jesus, in a sense, told Paul to get with the program and stop persecuting his people. In this incident, the Bible tells us that Jesus is already dead, and resurrected. This book argues otherwise. http://amzn.to/2zSDsuP $5.99 Kindle $19.95 softcover

Christianity on the Arch of Titus

This book explores the "persons" visible on the Triumphant Arch of Titus which is located in the heart of Rome. These people were significant in that they played a role, not only in Rome's conquest of Judaea but also in the creation of Christianity. This book explores those individuals and the roles they played in the creation of one of the most important religious movements in world history. https://amzn.to/3xz3OgM $3.69 Kindle 10.95 paperback.

www.robertvillegas.com

The Real Purpose-Driven Life

After centuries of being told that it is not about you, it is time to set the record straight. You are a unique individual and your goal in life should be to achieve your own happiness. This book is about helping you accomplish your goals and fixing your purpose firmly in place. It covers not only why you should pursue your goals but how to do it. https://amzn.to/3ebkhjr $3.99 Kindle $6.95 softcover

The Values and Purpose Workbook

Rather than give you tasks that involve doing a lot of things for other people, I'm am going to tell you that focusing on yourself will reveal your life's purpose and express your passions and freedom. I'm going to start with you. https://amzn.to/3eQf4wG $2.99 Kindle $6.95 softcover

This Book is About You

Some people move briskly bent on a purpose, concerned only about what they are about. People walk by them; they don't even notice. They just keep to their path and you wonder where they are going. This book is about you. It's about time. https://amzn.to/3vFMzss $6299 Kindle $5.95 softcover

www.robertvillegas.com

Existence a Rational Thoughtbook

A Rational Thoughtbook is designed for thinking as opposed to reading. It combines brief prescient content with stunning imagery. Existence focuses on the nature of existence and gives you intelligent thoughts to integrate into your life.

https://amzn.to/2RZpsKV $4.99 Kindle $12.95 softcover

The Virtue of Independence

One of the most important goals for any person is to establish intellectual independence. Intellectual independence is the road to "life" independence, which is the ability to earn your own way without help from others. https://amzn.to/3awuCV2 $2.99 Kindle $6.95 softcover

Rational Meditation

Rational Meditation is self-meditation. It is thinking about yourself without guilt and without the tenets of modern philosophy (that the world is unknowable, that man is a phony, that ethics and living are only about others). https://amzn.to/3gus9OE $6.99 Kindle $12.95 softcover

History of My Mind

This booklet is the companion to my book entitled Rational Meditation. It utilizes the various exercises of the original book that involve contemplation or meditation and provide space for written input by the reader. https://amzn.to/3gy3hpl $4.69 Kindle $11.95 softcover.

www.robertvillegas.com

Existence a Rational Thoughtbook

A Rational Thoughtbook is designed for thinking as opposed to reading. It combines brief prescient content with stunning imagery. Existence focuses on the nature of existence and gives you intelligent thoughts to integrate into your life.
https://amzn.to/2RZpsKV $4.99 Kindle $12.95 softcover

Identity

One of the most important goals for any person is to establish intellectual independence. Intellectual independence is the road to "life" independence, which is the ability to earn your own way without help from others. https://amzn.to/3nf9aJn $3.99 Kindle $9.95 softcover

www.robertvillegas.com

Fiction and Creative Poems and Plays

Poetic Prose and Poetry

These expressions represent some of Mr. Villegas' deepest thoughts as he lived and traveled throughout the world in locations such as Germany (East and West), Austria, Britain, Spain, Canada, France, Luxembourg, Belgium, the Netherlands, Korea, New York, Miami, San Francisco and other locations. https://amzn.to/3vu7X3B $2.99 Kindle $6.95 softcover

The Lost Poems

These poems were discovered among Mr. Villegas's archives in 2016. Many of them have been read by only Mr. Villegas. Most of these poems were rejected as "not that good". After seeing them again, he has changed his mind. These poems expressive, fresh and spontaneously honest. https://amzn.to/3aPg5nB $3.99 Kindle $6.95 softcover

Adam Reborn – A Short Play

Adam Reborn is a play of symbols. Adam and Eve, as I have portrayed them, are young and heroic people learning to deal with a Paradise and God that are hostile to them. There is no chance of life for them. https://amzn.to/3u9Nr8b $2.99 Kindle $6.95 softcover

The Boy Who Stood Alone

Jonny Payne has just discovered Ayn Rand and his parents don't know what to do. They take him to a priest and a psychologist but his only question is "What is the price of independence? https://amzn.to/3nCG6ve $3.99 Kindle $6.95 paperback.

www.robertvillegas.com

Fiction and Creative Materials

Aphrodite

Johnny is a Spanish guitar player with a mysterious past. At a party, he meets the beautiful songstress Aphrodite who is enthralled with his flamenco guitar skills. Later, she learns they have a connection, a particular song they both appear to know. Aphrodite discovers the connection, and through dreams, the two fall in love. The question is whether they will ever be together. https://amzn.to/3xIlmXZ $3.99 Kindle $5.95 softcover

The Odyssey of Amerigo the Founder

Amerigo was born in a time of desperation and dystopia. He was the only man with the vision of a great future. Many repaired to his cause while others swore to destroy him. They wanted his life, his mind and everything he loved. He swore that no matter what they did, he would win the struggle for freedom and a new future. https://amzn.to/2Qz8h2t $3.99 Kindle $8.95 softcover

Bob and Bobbie

1967 - a town outside Camp Casey, Korea - two young people have come together to challenge a world that makes love impossible. https://amzn.to/3sZWSpf $2.99 Kindle $5.95 softcover

The Raven Haired Girl

Bobby met Angie 52 years ago in a poor neighborhood in Indianapolis. It was love at first sight. For a few short months, their relationship blossomed into love. They were in love but didn't know how to be in love because they were only fourteen years old. https://amzn.to/3306plF $2.99 Kindle $6.95 paperback.

www.robertvillegas.com

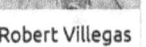
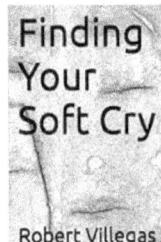

Naming Names in the NT

"Discovery consists of seeing what everybody has seen and thinking what nobody has thought." - Albert Szent-Gyogyi – 1937 Nobel Laureate

https://amzn.to/3mXR66H $3.99 Kindle $9.95 softcover $16.95 hardcover

Finding Your Soft Cry

Every individual has a yearning to know that he is both free and good. This yearning comes to him from early youth, and he hopes that he eventually develops the intellectual tools to help him distinguish between his nature and the demands of society. The key to freedom is the ability to act without restriction and, especially, without guilt. https://amzn.to/3p8lY7m $3.99 Kindle $8.95 softcover $15.95 hardcover

The New Totalitarianism – Quo Vadis?

The previous century was one of the bloodiest in history. Two World Wars and many other wars do not bode well for our century that is beginning to rival the previous in its bloodlust. If we look carefully, we find in the last century the philosophical roots of the present century. The philosophers of the last century are the philosophers of the present. https://amzn.to/3AMZNFC $5.99 Kinde $10.95 softcover $25.95 hard cover

A Call to Reason

Is it possible that the problems in the world are not caused by capitalism and rich people? Is it possible that anti-capitalism and anti-reason philosophies are nothing more than elaborate hoaxes designed to convince people to give up everything they have honestly earned and take it away from them? Is it possible they are caused by the re-distribution of capital to wasteful uses and the consequent destruction of jobs and affluence? https://amzn.to/3mVNrq5 $5.99 Kindle $9.95 softcover $24.95 Hardcover

www.robertvillegas.com

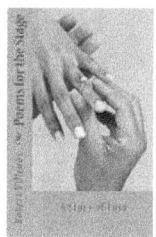 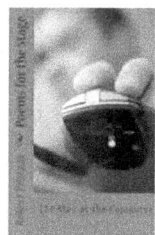

Poems for the Stage – A Story of Love

This dramatic presentation features poems found in Mr. Villegas's book Poetic Prose and Poetry. Some are also found in his book.

https://amzn.to/3gSJctV $2.99 Kindle $5.95 softcover

Poems for the Stage – The Man at the Computer

This dramatic presentation is based upon poems from Mr. Villegas's book Poetic Prose and Poetry. Some of the poems have been slightly altered to reflect the internal story. Mr. Villegas's book Poetic Prose and Poetry can be found on Amazon.com.

https://amzn.to/2R8zpFf $2.99 Kindle $5.95 softcover

www.robertvillegas.com

A Boomer takes on the Far Left

I just learned something about myself – and it isn't very good. In fact, it is very bad. I learned that the opinions of Boomers don't matter any more. We are obsolete in this new age of new knowledge. Anything we think is unimportant and false. I don't think so. https://amzn.to/3tzNqtc $5.19 Kindle $10.95 softcover

Crushing the Alinsky Radicals

The worst enemy of individual rights today is a group of people I call the Alinsky Radicals. These people are now in charge of our culture and temporarily, in charge of government. They are associated, philosophically and politically, with the communists and fascists of the past. They are not your father's liberals. They are the direct descendants of dictators such as Stalin and Mao. In this book, I hope to convince you of the evil of the Alinsky Radicals and to provide the intellectual ammunition you need to eradicate them from society. https://amzn.to/3hbh9WN $3.49 Kindle $8.95 softcover

The Conservative's Dilemma

I wrote this book to ask some important questions about the conservative philosophy of altruism. https://amzn.to/3bfDQ8e $2.99 Kinde $6.95 softcover.

The Biggest Mistakes in History – 2008 to 2016

To be the Chief Executive of the greatest country in the world requires a leader with a great deal of knowledge, experience and reasoning ability. It requires having the very best minds as advisors, minds that the President can count on to give reasoned arguments and detailed knowledge about the important issues of the day. I think it takes a special ability to understand the principle of cause and effect concerning how government action impacts the lives of real people. https://amzn.to/3tDQ4OI $2.99 Kindle $10.95 softcover

www.robertvillegas.com

Dachau and Berlin in 1990

This booklet chronicles Mr. Villegas' thoughts during visits to Dachau and Berlin during 1990, disclosing my observations of milestones in German history, past and present, and relating those events to world happenings as they were unfolding at the time. I traveled throughout Germany for much of 1990 while on business. https://amzn.to/3ex578d $2.99 Kindle $6.95 softcover

What Harvard and Princeton Don't Want You to Know

The professors at Harvard and Princeton don't want you to know about the worst ideas in history. This is because they have been pawning these ideas off as true and profound. They have been using them to deceive and manipulate us for centuries. https://amzn.to/3farP5p $5.19 Kindle $9.95 softcover

Defending American Values

This book is made up of several chapters about American values and how they can be defended without a descent into the abyss of dictatorship. The book argues for individual rights and provides reasons why we should fight for them. https://amzn.to/3uMFq9L $3.99 Kinde $5.95 softcover.

Capitalism Doesn't Fail

How many times have we heard the old saw: "Capitalism has failed again" over the course of contemporary events? We heard it during the Great Depression of 1929 after Hoover had invoked tariffs and precipitated economic retaliation and a banking crisis. Along with this question usually came a statement to the effect, that "We can fix capitalism and make it even stronger by issuing economic controls or spending money to stimulate economic activity." This book will argue that capitalism, as an economic system, cannot fail as long as individuals are free to act. https://amzn.to/3xZIAJ6 $4.19 Kindle $10.95 softcover

www.robertvillegas.com

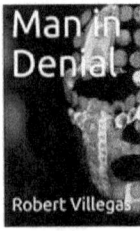   

Man in Denial

If psychology has no solid epistemology and metaphysics, how can it stand on its own? I do not think it can and this explains why psychology is in such a sad state today. Yet, before we can put psychology on a solid foundation, philosophy too must advance above the level of puberty. With its base in modern philosophy, even philosophy cannot stand on its own which exposes the real problems with modern psychology. https://amzn.to/3oVTDAQ $5.99 Kindle $9.95 softcover $18.95 hardcover

Understanding the Modern Mind

The purpose of this book is to delve into critical issues about how the human mind has come to the modern position of doubt and despair. The culprits in this matter include the irrationality of both rationalism and skepticism, and, in particular, the child of skepticism known as pragmatism.
https://amzn.to/3mRLZF9 $6.99 Kindle $9.60 softcover $26.95 hardcover

How Marcuse Destroyed Capitalism

One of the fathers of critical theory was Herbert Marcuse who escaped European dictatorship only by coming to America. America gave him the freedom and protection he needed to destroy capitalism in America.
https://amzn.to/2YW9LaS $4.99 Kinde $8.95 softcover.

The Logical Fallacy of Altruism

A logical fallacy is a faulty thought process that violates a rule of proper thinking. Correct arguments are defined as proper generalized expressions that define logical truths or knowledge. In effect, a rule of logical reasoning addresses all of the common modes of valid argument while the faulty argument contradicts them. This book examines altruism as a logical fallacy.
https://amzn.to/3vdFiB0 $5.99 Kindle $9.95 softcover $18.95 Hardcover

www.robertvillegas.com

Finding Sponsors 1 and 2

This book is written for anyone seeking sponsorship relationships in the sport and entertainment fields. The ideas and principles presented here are applicable to any company, sport team, entertainment company, marketing agency and charitable organization that uses corporate sponsorships to support its activities. Volume 1: https://amzn.to/3ejm1Hp $5.19 Kindle $12.95 softcover Volume 2: https://amzn.to/3eVDo0e $4.69 Kindle $10.95 softcover

How to Write a Sponsorship Proposal

This booklet provide you with some basic guidelines on what to communicate in order to produce a winning sponsorship proposal. These guidelines will focus on what you should be presenting to your potential sponsor to make the best business case for involvement with your team or entertainment company. $2.99 Kindle $6.95 softcover

Hospitality Event Planning Handbook

One key part of your sponsorship activation strategy might be customer hospitality events in conjunction with sporting events. How do you pull off a Hospitality Event for your biggest customers? You may not know how to start, what to do and how to ensure the event is a success. This book can help. http://amzn.to/2mxzpgy $7.95 softcover.

Selling Sponsorship in the Age of the Coronavirus

This book provides suggestions on how sport teams, athletes and concert promoters can mitigate the damage done to their businesses by the economic lockdowns (due to the Coronavirus). It integrates checklists, SWOT Analysis and other valuable business aids into one toolkit that will help you keep your sport and/or genre alive in these difficult times. https://amzn.to/2QVBNiM $5.15 Kindle $5.95 softcover

www.robertvillegas.com

Finding Sponsors Forms Book

This "Forms Book" is intended to provide samples of the forms mentioned in my book "Finding Sponsors for Sport and Entertainment". This will make it possible for you to reproduce these forms in other formats as well as download the forms document from the SponsorProAZ website for use with Microsoft Word. https://amzn.to/3b95yDW $2.99 Kindle $5.50 softcover

Submitting Your Sponsorship Proposal Online

This booklet enables sport teams and concert promoters to submit their sponsorship proposals to companies that accept only online submission of proposals. https://amzn.to/3euzdti $2.99 Kindle $5.95 softcover

The Art of Sponsorship

This short book is based upon Mr. Villegas' book "Finding Sponsors for Sport and Entertainment". It is also based upon a course that he taught for an organization managing Indiana Parks and Recreation facilities. It is, in a sense, a condensation of information from the book geared toward organizations that would like to earn revenues on their facilities through corporate sponsorship. https://amzn.to/3beuVnC $2.99 Kinde $6.95 softcover.

Restarting Your Business After the Pandemic

This new book is designed to help you restart your business after the Coronavirus pandemic. You will find here all the right questions, how you can find the answers and the forms you need to walk through your restart and coming success. https://amzn.to/2QVBNiM $5.15 Kindle $5.95 softcover

www.robertvillegas.com